CRIME AND DETECTION

THE WAR AGAINST DRUGS

Crime and Detection series

- Criminal Terminology
- Cyber Crime
- Daily Prison Life
- Death Row and Capital Punishment
- Domestic Crime
- Famous Prisons
- Famous Trials
- Forensic Science
- Government Intelligence Agencies
- Hate Crimes
- The History and Methods of Torture
- The History of Punishment
- International Terrorism
- Major Unsolved Crimes
- Organized Crime
- Protecting Yourself Against Criminals
- Race and Crime
- Serial Murders
- The United States Justice System
- The War Against Drugs

JUL   2004

CRIME AND DETECTION

THE WAR AGAINST DRUGS

MICHAEL KERRIGAN

MASON CREST PUBLISHERS
www.masoncrest.com

Mason Crest Publishers Inc.
370 Reed Road
Broomall, PA 19008
(866) MCP-BOOK (toll free)
www.masoncrest.com

First printing

1 2 3 4 5 6 7 8 9 10

Library of Congress Cataloging-in-Publication Data on file at the Library of Congress

ISBN 1-59084-368-1

Editorial and design by
Amber Books Ltd.
Bradley's Close
74–77 White Lion Street
London N1 9PF
www.amberbooks.co.uk

Project Editor: Michael Spilling
Design: Floyd Sayers
Picture Research: Natasha Jones

Printed and bound in Malaysia

Picture credits
Corbis: 66; DEA Museum, Washington, D.C.: 15; Popperfoto: 6, 10, 12, 14, 24, 32, 33, 41, 44–45, 49, 53, 59, 64, 75, 89; Topham Picturepoint: 11, 13, 16, 18, 20, 21, 22, 23, 25, 26, 27, 28, 30, 31, 35, 36, 38, 39, 42, 43, 37, 39, 46, 50, 51, 54, 56, 61, 63, 65, 68, 69, 72, 73, 78, 82, 84, 85, 87; U.S. Coast Guard: 8, 57, 76, 79, 81, 83, 86.
Front cover: Popperfoto.

CONTENTS

Introduction

From the moment in the Book of Genesis when Cain's envy of his brother Abel erupted into violence, crime has been an inescapable feature of human life. Every society ever known has had its own sense of how things ought to be, its deeply held views on how men and women should behave. Yet in every age there have been individuals ready to break these rules for their own advantage: they must be resisted if the community is to thrive.

This exciting and vividly illustrated series of books sets out the history of crime and detection from the earliest times to the present day, from the empires of the ancient world to the towns and cities of the 21st century. From the commandments of the great religions to the theories of modern psychologists, it considers changing attitudes toward offenders and their actions. Contemporary crime is examined in its many different forms: everything from racial hatred to industrial espionage, from serial murder to drug trafficking, from international terrorism to domestic violence.

The series looks, too, at the heroic work of those men and women entrusted with the task of overseeing and maintaining law and order, from judges and court officials to police officers and other law enforcement agents. The tools and techniques at their disposal are described in detail, and the ethical issues they face are concisely and clearly explained.

All in all, the *Crime and Detection* series provides a comprehensive and accessible account of this exciting world, in theory and in practice, past and present.

CHARLIE FULLER

Executive Director, International Association of Undercover Officers

Left: Here, a Thai soldier destroys opium poppies in Thailand's northern Chiang Rai Province, close to neighboring Laos and Myanmar. This area is commonly known as the "Golden Triangle," and is one of the world's biggest traditional opium-producing centers.

In the War Zone

To speak of a "war" against drugs may sound exaggerated, yet there can be little doubt that drugs have been at war with us for over a generation now. Any of our historical enemies would have been proud of a military offensive that recorded the many hundreds of casualties claimed each year by the use of illicit drugs, not to mention the many thousands killed as a result of drug-related crime. Waves of bomber aircraft, massed in thousands, pounded Europe's cities into rubble in the dark days of World War II: all it took here was a few street-corner drug-dealers and their clients.

IN THE WAR ZONE

What "rogue state" would not dream of disrupting our economy to the tune of $100 billion a year? By some estimates, that is what the trade in drugs has been costing the United States. In one respect, the term "war on drugs" is misleading, in the sense that it does not go far enough. For typical wars have always had the effect of mobilizing, even inspiring, the American people. No human foe has ever succeeded in demoralizing whole communities in the way that drugs have, miring so many thousands in indifference and defeatism.

It is really no exaggeration to say that the United States has never faced a clearer or more present danger than this one. It is time for us all to rally to the defense of our nation.

Left: Another shipment stopped, another job well done, but these U.S. Customs agents in Saint Petersburg, Florida, are in no mood for self-congratulation. They are only too well aware of the staggering volumes of illegal drugs streaming into the United States each day, moved by ruthless and well-organized "narcotrafficking" gangs. Coast Guard, Customs, and Border Patrol agents have to be ever vigilant to stem the tide of illegal substances entering the United Staes.

Casualties lie strewn about the battlefields that our inner cities have become, with whole communities caught up in a war without glory. Despair, degradation—and ultimately even death: these are the destiny to which drugs have brought too many Americans.

A world away from the alley or the crack house, cigar aficionados in New York enjoy the glamor and excitement of a celebratory "smoke-in." Yet all drugs exact a price: however rich or "respectable" we may be, we should all think hard about the risks we may be running in the name of having fun.

INNER-CITY APOCALYPSE

A knot of young people laughs and jokes on a corner: just boys having fun or a robbery in waiting? The respectable citizen scarcely knows what to think or which way to look. A harassed-looking mother hurries by, eyes down, her children stumbling after her. Every second on these streets, it seems, is an ordeal. Remembering the days when this was just like any other urban community, the elderly move about, blinking as though disbelieving the sight that meets their eyes. It is not an attractive scene: 20th-century high-rise buildings stand like medieval ruins; the surrounding buildings stand derelict or have been cleared from these scorched-earth wastelands. This neighborhood has no function now but the nurturing of criminal acts.

Drug-related crime tarnishes society: here in Mexico City, the power of the drug gangs means that even the law has to hide its face as federal agents stand guard over a changing house that is thought to have been used by cocaine smugglers for money laundering.

This is, apparently, America. Indeed, just a few minutes' walk away, men and women work in light and airy offices, relax in clean and friendly cafés, and do their shopping in elegant and spacious malls. But that world might as well be a million miles away. The only visitors who ever make it down here from "planet uptown" are those drivers who patrol these curbs looking to buy a young body for a few dollars.

IT IS NOT JUST HAPPENING IN THE U.S.

The Farmer's Arms pub in Fazakerley, north Liverpool, in England, was crowded as Stephen Cole sat drinking with his wife, but no witnesses could be found to what then happened. As far as can be established, a couple of carloads of thugs drew up outside, sauntered into the bar, and attacked Cole, a club doorman, with machetes.

Cole's was just the latest death in a spiral of revenge killings that had gripped this city with fear. A once-great seaport in decline for decades, Liverpool had always had a reputation for casual violence and crime, but the emergence of the city as a center for the European drug trade in the 1990s brought a new and frightening culture of violence and intimidation. Who is in charge in Liverpool now? Local law enforcement has been pleading for government assistance in taking on the drug gangs, who are far better funded, armed, and equipped than the police.

IMPOVERISHING US ALL

The costs of America's drug problem are counted far beyond our obviously disadvantaged inner cities. The indirect effects have an influence on every man, woman, and child living in the U.S. today. In January 2002, the White House Office of National Drug Control Policy (ONDCP) reported that illicit drug use was costing an estimated $160,000 a year to the U.S. economy. The costs include those of providing health care treatment for addicts and social support for their dependents. Then there is the cost of law enforcement measures demanded by increasing levels of drug-related crime. The victims of violent attacks by addicts, like those caught in the crossfire in drug-related gangland conflicts (as well as the criminals themselves), require medical treatment at a huge expense to the U.S. economy.

Men and women who become victims of drug-related crime often have to take time off from work, and this also represents a major cost to the economy. Far greater, however, is that cost represented by the imprisonment of so many young people at what should be the most productive period of their lives. The truth is that, by any measure—whether that of human misery or economic cost—drug abuse clearly represents a colossal waste of American energy and potential.

WHERE IS THIS PLACE?

The scene described is in downtown Detroit, although it could be almost any other American inner city, from Baltimore to Los Angeles, from South Bronx to East St. Louis: all these places stand on the frontline in the war against drugs. While drugs are not the only problem in these places—Detroit, for instance, has been hit hard in recent decades by a slump in the U.S. auto industry—the influence of drugs and drug-related crime in transforming communities into urban wastelands of this kind cannot be denied. **Illicit** drugs, when not killers themselves, often cause the deaths of those who deal in them, as well as of innocent bystanders who find

Another young African American is picked up to join the city-sized population that is already behind bars: the African-American community has perhaps suffered more than any other from the impact of illegal drugs in the United States.

Eleven tons of captured cocaine go up in smoke in a forest clearing, another score for U.S. agencies working with the Colombian government. The war on drugs is fought not only on the streets of America's cities, but also in producing countries, from South America to the Far East.

themselves caught between the desperate **addict**, and his or her daily fix.

Thousands of lively, talented teenagers have been drawn into a gang culture that dooms them—if they are lucky—to the incalculable waste of a life in prison. Drug addiction has bred a whole generation of "crack babies"—babies born already addicted to this drug because their mothers smoked crack while pregnant. So many young Americans find themselves trapped in this horrific world because of their communities' dependence on drugs and the money drugs bring. The cycle of drug addiction and the crime and hopelessness it brings seems almost inescapable at times.

NO LONGER THE LAND OF THE FREE

If the cities and people described seem strange to most Americans, that is not necessarily surprising, for these people can hardly be seen as being Americans in the fullest sense of the word. For hundreds of years, freedom has been the defining American value and, caught in their cycle of drug dependency, these Americans could never be described as being "free."

It has been said that Americans can make of themselves whatever they want; no such possibilities exist for those trapped in the terrible world of our drug-ridden inner cities. Yet drugs are not just a problem of impoverished inner cities. Young people in suburban areas and small towns are also at risk of being sucked into the hopelessness and crime that drug addiction all-too-often represents.

The damage done by illegal drug use is most apparent on the crime-ravaged streets of our inner cities, and yet all Americans are affected, at least indirectly. Even the most prosperous communities see their quality of living adversely affected by the need to guard against auto theft and other drug-related crimes; any one of us may fall victim to street robbery or to burglary at home. The war against drugs is, therefore, a fight for the right of all Americans to live free from a crippling dependency and paralyzing fear. It is a war that, when all is said and done, our society simply cannot afford to lose.

The Enemy

Drugs are often talked about as though they are a single problem, rather than a wide variety of different substances, each with its own chemical properties, physiological effects, dangers, and attractions. Heroin, cocaine, cannabis, amphetamines, and ecstasy all pose quite different problems and they are often taken by quite different kinds of people. There are other drugs, too, which, however harmful, society has decided to accept: alcohol and nicotine being the two most obvious.

NARCOTICS

The term "narcotics" is often used to mean drugs in general, but, strictly speaking, it covers only one particular category of substances. These are noted for their capacity to kill pain, promote **euphoria**, and, unfortunately, for their addictive nature. The best-known examples are opiates, derived from certain poppies. This plant has been cultivated for countless centuries through much of southern and eastern Asia. Juice from its crushed seed pods is purified by repeated boiling before being reduced to a thick paste, which may be smoked as "opium." Sumerian texts dating from 3,000 years ago identify the poppy as the "plant of joy," although its properties may well have been discovered many centuries earlier. The structure of opiate molecules resembles the natural pain-relieving **endorphins** produced by the brain. This lets them "trick" the brain into a sense of blissful well-being. The ancient Greek poet Homer describes a drink, *nepenthe*, which "robbed grief and anger of their sting and banished painful memories." This is believed to have been opium dissolved in wine. A descendant of this drink,

Left: High society? An elegantly jeweled, manicured hand prepares lines of cocaine for use at a party: the air of sophistication surrounding many drugs may make the fight against their use that much more difficult.

A member of a Colombian Narcotics Brigade raids a field of opium poppies in a remote area: this plant, Asiatic in origin, was introduced to South America specifically to supply the illicit export trade to the United States.

called laudanum, was popular well into modern times, drunk by men and women from all sections of society in the 19th century.

Taking drugs has often been depicted as being somehow "artistic" or "glamorous," and this has been one of the great obstacles to the development of a sensible attitude toward drugs. The main opiate in use today is heroin, which tends to be injected. At first, because it had the reputation as a drug used for healing, this form of drug taking was exclusive to certain professionals, most notably those in the medical profession.

Today, of course, this is no longer the case, heroin addiction having taken hold among large sections of disadvantaged youth. In 1999, 208,000 Americans were estimated to be using heroin: their average age at first use was 21.

DRUG ADDICTS AND WITHDRAWAL SYMPTOMS

English writer Thomas de Quincey and poet Samuel Taylor Coleridge were famous opium users of their time, and their works were often seen later as advertisements for the "liberating" effects of the drug. In truth, however,

The Romantic poets and writers of the late 18th and early 19th centuries, including Samuel Taylor Coleridge (above), were eager to experiment with consciousness-altering drugs in their quest for literary inspiration.

the creativity of both men was tragically curtailed by their use of the drug. Coleridge described his own addiction as "the worst and most degrading of slaveries." Indeed, addicts find that after a certain point they are taking a drug not for the marvelous feelings they experienced, but simply to hold at bay the extremely unpleasant sensations of "withdrawal."

Any activity can be habit-forming when it becomes part of a person's routine and he or she starts to take psychological comfort from it and begins to consider it to be an aspect of everyday normality. In the case of many drugs, however, such habits can become far more deeply embedded in body and mind to the extent that serious "withdrawal symptoms" may

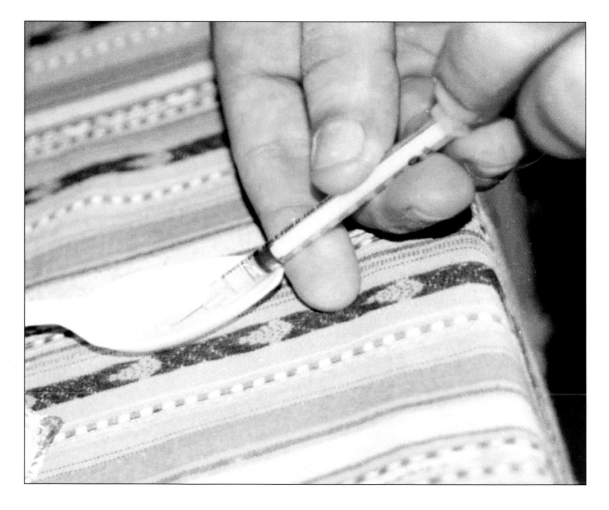

A heroin addict prepares to shoot up: quite apart from the ill-effects of the opiate itself, and the substances it is "cut" with, intravenous drug use may involve grave risks of cross-infection with a range of diseases, most especially AIDS.

The death of rock legend Jimi Hendrix in 1970, at the age of only 28, should be a warning to all young people. In reality, the opposite has been true: such tragedies only add to the romantic allure of drugs: for all our sakes, we must conquer our addiction to this dangerous mythology.

result when the routine is interrupted.

The problem is that even while the drug produces the instant effects the addict craves, it may also be causing more far-reaching changes. This is because the chemical balance in the brain adjusts itself to the presence of a drug and learns to accept it as normal. The development of this type of "tolerance" means that ever higher dosages are needed in order to achieve the same results, while the absence of the drug throws the brain into a sort of confusion that **debilitates** the addict.

UNFORESEEN CONSEQUENCES

The dangers of drugs are fearsome enough without a number of other hazards. One of the most dreadful of these is the risk of infection with AIDS. Myanmar (formerly Burma) is one corner of Southeast Asia's infamous opium-producing "Golden Triangle," and this country now has many hundreds of thousands of heroin addicts, intravenous injection having replaced more traditional (and safe) forms of getting high on opium. Addiction on such a scale is a tragedy in itself, but the practice of sharing needles has enabled the Human Immunodeficiency Virus—HIV—to spread like wildfire. The virus attacks those cells in the bloodstream and nervous system that would normally resist infection, leaving the body defenseless. It is believed that 3.46 percent of the Myanmar population has been affected (around 1.5 million people), a figure that is quickly rising.

"Just say no," said First Lady Nancy Reagan in a high-profile, yet controversial, campaign of the 1980s. Her critics argued that the complex issues of drug addiction could not be reduced to moral choices of such simplicity.

The effects can be dramatic and include **paranoia**, pain, nausea, and diarrhea, although the worst of these physical symptoms are generally over within a few days. The problem, however, is that the brain may take far longer to overcome its cravings completely. Drug-treatment experts believe it takes at least three years to overcome an addiction.

STIMULANTS

Any substance that excites the mind, increasing alertness and energy, is classified as a stimulant. The full list includes such everyday drugs as coffee, tea, and chocolate. The most important stimulants, however, are cocaine and amphetamines ("speed"), and using these can have alarming consequences.

Police prepare to destroy cocaine stocks seized at an illicit laboratory in the Colombian interior: an impressive find, yet there will be plenty more where this batch came from.

THE DEMON DRINK

Alcohol is a drug. Technically, it is known as an "inebriant"—a volatile chemical synthesis that acts rapidly and dramatically on the brain. It is related to chloroform, ether, and other solvents used by people addicted to sniffing glue. The fact that alcohol is widely accepted should not blind us to its powerfully addictive properties or the long-term damage it can do to the human body. Its impact on the health of society is arguably far more serious. Alcoholism wrecks individual lives and families. Department of Justice statistics estimate that alcohol plays a role in around 4 in 10 of all violent crimes recorded. For domestic violence, those figures skyrocket: alcohol is a factor in three-quarters of the attacks by husbands or wives. Outside the home, drunk drivers create bloodshed on the roads, where 4 out of 10 car accidents are reported to involve alcohol.

"DESIGNER DRUGS"

Drugs that have been designed in chemical laboratories in order to avoid legal bans on other substances are known as "designer drugs." PCP, also called "angel dust," was developed in the 1920s to reproduce the effects of barbiturates, which had been outlawed. More recently, a drug called ecstasy has been in style. Club-goers appreciate the sense of contentment and companionship it brings. However, there is every sign that long-term use can bring ugly consequences.

Cocaine is usually inhaled through the nose ("snorted"). In the 1970s, it was fashionable to "freebase" cocaine by inhaling the vapors from heated crystals through a water pipe. This presented the drug in a far more addictive form whose dangerous potency anticipated that of "crack" a few years later. Crack is a derivative of pure cocaine dissolved in water, mixed with baking soda, and then dried out. When smoked, crack produces an overwhelming "rush" to the brain in a matter of seconds. This euphoria, however, comes and goes over a period of a few minutes, leaving the user desperate for more.

That desperation has been demonstrated all too clearly in the crime statistics of our inner cities. As with the shift in heroin addiction from wealthy professionals to impoverished inner-city youth, the transition from cocaine to crack represents a clear move "down market" and a mark of the ruthless opportunism of the drug trade. For years, cocaine was the glamorous drug of the wealthy middle classes. When that trend seemed to be passing, crack appeared, developed for sale to the urban poor.

Stimulants can be overdone—just ask anyone who ever went around "wired" from drinking too many cups of coffee. But illicit stimulants can have more alarming effects. In addition to creating dependency, they can produce excessive mental agitation that causes strong psychotic disturbances. Amphetamines may produce symptoms identical to those of schizophrenia; even low-level users may find themselves caught up in sudden and inexplicable moods of high anxiety or gloom. And even though the "buzz" produced by stimulants seems to fight off fatigue and suppress the appetite, enabling superhuman work rates or around-the-clock partying, the body still pays the price in the long run.

HYPNOTIC DRUGS AND HALLUCINOGENS

Hypnotic drugs cause feelings of peace and sleepiness, and so they are often used as medical **sedatives** or in sleeping pills. Hypnotic drugs, especially barbiturates, are also taken for the mood of calm contentment they bring.

However, just as with other drugs, users soon find themselves having to take ever-increasing doses to achieve ever-diminishing effects.

Hallucinogens affect our perceptions in complex ways, which are barely understood even now. It seems that something in them mimics the effects of certain natural chemicals in the brain. In theory, the effects are agreeable and "consciousness-expanding." In reality, they can cause major psychotic disturbances and emotional problems.

Cannabis, or marijuana, is produced from the hemp plant. It is one of the mildest and most common hallucinogens. Its leaves, the sticky resin

Marijuana, cannabis, weed, grass, dope—it goes by innumerable names and may be taken in several different ways. Under whatever name and in whatever form they come, however, the various products of the hemp plant may be a good deal less benign than their users tend to believe.

A DRUG BY ANY NAME?

The chemical that keeps cigarette smokers lighting up, nicotine is one of the most addictive substances known to mankind. It is a mild stimulant, yet the long-term impact of nicotine is potentially devastating. Long centuries of popular usage have given tobacco a privileged place in Western society, otherwise this dangerous drug would have been banned.

Lung cancer, bronchitis, emphysema, and heart disease are just a few of the diseases commonly caused by smoking. Over 400,000 Americans are killed by such illnesses every year. And these diseases do not merely affect smokers. Disturbing evidence has also been emerging of their impact on families, friends, and co-workers. Over 3,000 deaths a year are now attributed to "passive smoking," or "secondhand smoke"—that is, people who are regularly exposed to other people's smoke fumes.

from its flowers, or its ground up seeds and stems all yield the compound tetrahydrocannabinol (THC). This chemical acts on the central nervous system, causing dizziness, disorientation, and a mild euphoria that may be relaxing, but can have serious long-term consequences. Other hallucinogens include

Those who actually grow the drugs are generally impoverished farmers just trying to get by: they would jump at the chance to make a more ethical living, like this Honduran woman growing organic coffee.

These young espresso-users do not exactly exude criminality, but caffeine has been forbidden in certain places and at certain times. Every society must order itself according to the situation in which it finds itself: it is absurd to argue that there should, therefore, be no rules at all.

mescaline (derived from a kind of cactus), "magic mushrooms," and other plants, and the artificially synthesized lysergic acid, or LSD.

ONE MAN'S DRUG

Critics of current drug policy point out that it is inconsistent. Caffeine, alcohol, and nicotine are all (often dangerous) drugs whose use is sanctioned by U.S. law. They point out that, strictly speaking, the middle-aged New England woman sipping tea on the patio and the junkie collapsed on the apartment stairway could both be called "drug users."

Cultural and historical factors help define which drugs will be permissible and which will not. For instance, coffee was banned by rulers

PEYOTE PIETY

Peyote, a kind of cactus, is believed to have been taken by certain Native American peoples up to 2,000 years before the arrival of Christopher Columbus. In modern scientific terms, it is a hallucinogen. Native Americans saw peyote as a "divine plant," and eating the flesh or drinking its juice was the centerpiece of important religious rituals. Followers of the peyote cult (which is followed by no fewer than 40 different native peoples) insist on the medical properties of this remarkable plant. At the most mundane level, it is claimed that, like a Western medication, it acts effectively against a wide variety of common ailments. For traditional believers, however, peyote's true powers are derived from its divine ability to put the individual's soul in spiritual contact with his or her ancestors.

in the Arab world in the 16th century. Now it is accepted without question, as are alcohol and tobacco. (There are signs, however, that smoking, after so many generations, is increasingly frowned upon.) Changing social contexts have their impact, too. Cocaine was advertised in 1885 as a toothache cure, and many substances that are now illegal were once easily available.

RELIGIOUS USE

Those arguing for the relaxation of our drug laws often draw attention to the honorable tradition of religious drug use. Certainly in, many cultures, mind-altering substances have helped religious people achieve spiritual enlightenment. Long before it appeared in the coffee shops of the Arabian cities, for instance, caffeine was used by Muslim mystics, or *sufi*, while the shamans of Siberia ate **soma** (from a type of mushroom) to take them into their religious trances. However, what made sense in a Siberian village in former centuries has no bearing on what would be a sensible thing to do in a modern American suburb, especially now that we are fully aware of the consequences of such drugs.

Hippies in the spirit of the 1960s "counterculture," the Rainbow Family is dedicated to the pursuit of peace, love, and a mystic—sometimes drug-assisted—harmony with nature's rhythms. Here an elder prepares peyote at a gathering in an Oregon forest.

Fighting Back

The fight against drug abuse in the United States really began in the second half of the 19th century, when a series of increasingly restrictive laws were passed. Unfortunately, the effectiveness of such legislation was limited by confusion in the minds of the politicians and the public alike over what "drugs" were and precisely why their use should be controlled.

We have already seen the difficulty in drawing a clear line between those substances that should be tolerated and those that should be banned, but this is not the only problem. People tend to crave the perceived excitement associated with taking drugs, even as they jump back from the horrific self-destructiveness of the habit. Another problem has been the manner in which people have campaigned against drugs; at times, all they achieved was the weakening of their case in the eyes of a skeptical public. There has also been a persistent tendency to consider drugs as a menace inflicted by one race on another. This is a view that is quite rightly rejected by the vast majority of decent Americans.

EARLY EFFORTS

The first significant attempt to take hold of America's drug problem was the Pharmacy Act of 1868, which required the registration of people dispensing drugs in communities across the U.S. After these sensible beginnings, unfortunately, the antidrug crusade implemented a series of measures obviously targeted at the Chinese-American community, which was generally resented at this time on racial grounds. One by one, between

Left: Interrupting the supply of drugs is less important than suppressing the demand for them. Ideally, Americans would reject them of their own accord. The government's DARE (Drug Abuse Resistance Education) program aims to catch grade-school students like these when young.

1875 and 1890, the western states took steps to prohibit the opening of opium dens. Their real purpose, however, was to prevent Chinese Americans from getting together as a community. Smoking opium was clearly harmful, but few believed that this was the legislators' real concern.

Sadly, such actions set the antidrug cause back by several generations. The Harrison Narcotics Act of 1914, however, was more even-handed in the restrictions it imposed on the import and distribution of opium,

A man rolls a joint using a fresh marijuana leaf, his habit apparently as "natural" and liberating as the American outdoors. U.S. drug laws may seem at times to conflict with constitutionally guaranteed liberties, yet our freedoms have to be limited in the interests of society as a whole.

Dope smokers insist on the harmlessness of their habit, yet, quite apart from evidence that it may lead to other, more dangerous drugs, marijuana is quite capable of causing long-term damage all on its own.

cocaine, and their derivatives. On the face of it, it appeared to impose no restriction whatsoever, being concerned simply with the registering and taxing of imports. But its stipulation that a doctor could issue drugs "in the course of his professional practice only" was interpreted as meaning that addicts, not being officially "sick," could not legally be supplied as they had been previously.

The issues of drugs and race were often confused by early antidrug campaigners in ways that have not been easy for their successors to live down. The close association of anti-opium actions in the late 19th century and the "yellow peril" hysteria of the time left a long-standing legacy of suspicion among the Chinese-American community.

In the same way, in the early 20th century, the link made between smoking marijuana and the African-American community did much to discredit the campaigners' message in the long-term. Few respectable sources went so far as one newspaper, which claimed marijuana was "responsible for the raping of white women by crazed Negroes," but many expressed equally ugly opinions, albeit in more guarded terms. Even today, stereotypical ideas of Latinos as drug **traffickers** are widely prevalent, doing a grave injustice to the vast majority of that population and helping to give the antidrug message a bad name.

The first concerted drive against drugs as a national menace came with the formation of the Federal Bureau of Narcotics (FBN) by President Herbert Hoover in 1930. The charismatic Harry J. Anslinger was placed in

INTOXICATING RHETORIC

The tendency of some antidrug campaigners to get high on their own indignation could hardly be better highlighted than in the case of Harry J. Anslinger. A charismatic man, he may have delighted some in white America with many of his speeches, but as far as others were concerned, they were a big turn-off. Anslinger's infamous claim in 1929 that "reefer [marijuana] makes darkies think they're as good as white men" was never going to impress African-American—or enlightened, intelligent white—opinion. Where his comments were not outrageously offensive, they were often simply ludicrous, as with his insistence that "if the hideous monster Frankenstein came face to face with the monster marijuana, he would die of fright." The main effect of such absurd claims was to discredit the antidrug message altogether in the eyes of many young Americans, blinding them to the real dangers posed by illicit drug use.

charge. His strategy was one of reaching out to the source of the drugs to stop the traffic, with checks on ports and cooperation with agencies abroad. In partnership with foreign law enforcement, he launched collaborative operations and information exchanges that scored important successes over the course of the next few years.

President Herbert Hoover addresses an open-air rally in Washington, D.C. in 1932. It was arguably Hoover who opened the hostilities in what would come to be known as the "war on drugs," establishing strategies and tactics that have remained in use to this day.

The "hippies" of the 1960s took delight in outraging respectable America in every way they conceivably could: in the songs they sang, the clothes they wore, the values they proclaimed, and—perhaps above all—their open drug-use.

At first, the emphasis was on opium and cocaine, but concerns about marijuana were growing steadily. In 1937, marijuana was banned and made the target of a fierce campaign. Once again, however, real issues at hand became confused. It was true that migrant workers from Mexico often imported marijuana, but the campaign of harsh criticism against Mexicans as spreaders of the "marijuana epidemic" was tainted with racial prejudice.

FLOWER POWER

The pattern established by Anslinger and his agency in the 1930s more or less continued through the postwar years, although traffickers seemed to be getting better at sidestepping security measures. Cocaine and heroin use continued to rise steadily even though the law was toughened up by the Boggs Act (1951) and the Narcotic Control Act (1956). These problems came to a head with the "counterculture" of the 1960s, which saw an explosion of interest in drugs on the part of educated and otherwise law-abiding young Americans. Young "hippies" liked to take drugs, both for their supposedly "mind-expanding" properties and (perhaps even more) as an act of defiance against a middle-aged, middle-class American establishment.

In 1965, in response to this enormous rise in drug use, and the fact that the use of amphetamine stimulants and hallucinogens was rapidly on the rise, a larger Bureau of Drug Abuse Control (BDAC) was formed within the Food and Drugs Administration (FDA). This agency merged with the FBN in 1968 to form the Bureau of Narcotics and Dangerous Drugs (BNDD). All federal antidrug forces were brought together into the Drug Enforcement Administration (DEA) in 1973.

COUNTERCULTURE CAPITAL

Hippie culture never died out in Amsterdam, Netherlands, where marijuana is freely available in "coffee shops" (pictured). But the city's liberal laws on the use of "soft drugs" (as opposed to "hard

drugs") have certainly not freed it from the problems posed by hard drugs. In fact, such liberal laws have seen the Netherlands emerge as a regional hub for the international illegal drug trade.

Opium

Opium has been used as a drug for countless centuries, but it is only in relatively recent times that it has become a global problem. The economic and political roots of our current drug wars can be traced back to the 19th century, at a time when Western powers like Britain were stamping their imperial authority on the world. Their attempts to modernize agricultural production of every kind had deep consequences. Until then, opium production had been a strictly local industry, but new labor practices helped it develop into a mass-commodity to be exported far and wide.

Today, a number of Asian countries know that they simply could not do without the revenues the drug trade brings in, despite official protestations of disapproval. Like it or not, opium is a factor in world politics and economics today. For this reason, America's war on drugs is fought on two fronts. Clamping down on users and dealers at home is one half of the battle. Reaching out to the

Here, more than 200 million dollars' worth of opium, heroin, and marijuana are burned during an Interpol drug conference in Yangon, Myanmar (formerly Burma), in 1999.

Here, a Burmese woman smokes opium in the early 20th century. For centuries, opium has been prized for its medicinal virtues. Only relatively recently has the drug been abused. Today, the Laos–Thailand–Burma "Golden Triangle" is economically addicted to opium, while thousands of its people are chemically hooked on heroin.

producing countries, offering support in finding alternative sources of income, is the other half.

THE WAR FOR DRUGS?

The assumption made by white Westerners in the late 19th century that opium was an aspect of an imaginary Chinese "yellow peril" was particularly unjust in light of that people's recent history. Though opium had long been familiar in China, and throughout Asia, it had been eaten medicinally rather than smoked as a recreational drug. Under its Manchu emperors, China turned its back on the outside world, shunning both diplomatic and commercial contact. As the 19th century began, however, a Britain booming because of its Industrial Revolution was looking far and wide for export markets and for sources of raw materials.

Britain had an imperial base in India, where it was modernizing agriculture, in particular, producing thousands of tons of opium, for which it then had to find a market. By the 1830s, the excess of Indian opium was damaging not just China's trade balance, but also the morale of what, in coastal areas, was fast becoming a population of addicts. In an attempt to protect his people, the emperor imposed restrictions on opium imports. Britain complained that "free trade" was being impeded and set out to reinstate it by armed force. This meant that from 1839 to 1843 and again between 1856 and 1860, Britain has the dubious distinction of being the only imperial power to have gone to war on behalf of the international drug trade.

The "Opium Wars" had their positive consequences, opening up China to economic development, but the negative impact of British victory was every bit as bad as the emperor had feared. Opium smoking became a sort of national addiction among the Chinese, leaving them unable to take advantage of the other economic modernizations the wars had brought. In 1852, meanwhile, Britain began the sale of opium to the populace of its latest imperial possession, Burma, an action that would cause trouble for both Britain and the West in general in times to come.

Along with Laos and Thailand, Burma (now Myanmar) is one corner of the "Golden Triangle," one of the most important opium-producing regions of the world. Today, Myanmar alone has over 220,000 acres under cultivation with opium poppies, yielding about 1,000 tons of opium per year, according to CIA estimates. It is surpassed as a producer only by Afghanistan, which has a smaller cultivated area (127,200 acres), but a higher yield. Estimates suggest 1,670 metric tons were produced in 1999.

Opium has also traditionally been produced over the Afghan border in Pakistan. Here, the authorities have been cooperating with the U.S. government in plans to destroy crops and find new forms of economic activity for local people. A newcomer in the field has been Colombia, for a long time associated mainly with cocaine, but whose drug barons have recently diversified into producing drugs of other kinds. Here, too, in partnership with the national government, the U.S. has led the way in developing two-pronged strategies for tackling opium cultivation, applying the benefit of developmental aid alongside the threat of military action against producers.

FROM FIELD TO STREET

Opium is harvested from the poppies as a sticky juice, which trickles out and can be collected through skillfully made slits in the growing seed pods. Once dried to a brownish color, the resulting gum is boiled in water to remove impurities. The water is then boiled off, and the opium is considered "cooked," ready for smoking or eating in the traditional manner.

However, it is not pure enough to be injected. The morphine from which heroin will be derived is only one of over 30 different chemical compounds present in this dark brown opium paste, so it has to be separated out in a laboratory. Here, the mixture is boiled in water again, but this time lime is added. This lets the insoluble morphine be drawn off as water-soluble calcium morphenate. Once this solution has been drained off

Peruvian law-enforcement agents consign another bag to the flames: in July 2001, no less than 3.5 tons of captured drugs were destroyed, ranging from marijuana and cocaine to opium, morphine, and unprocessed poppy.

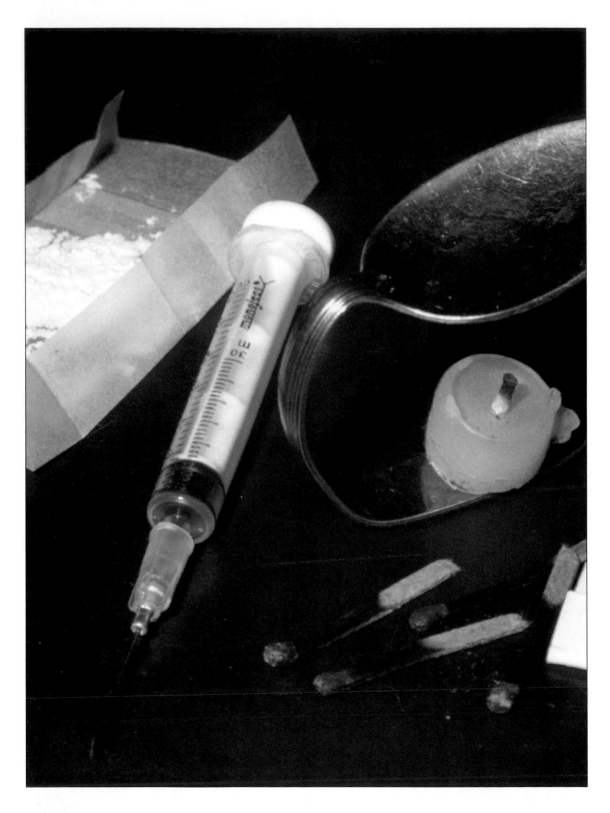

A heroin addict's "works," including a bent-spoon arrangement for melting the heroin powder down into liquid form—and, of course, the syringe with which it will actually be injected into the bloodstream.

It is hard (and unreasonable) to persuade poor peasants to consider the problems of the world's richest country: few can imagine the toll their harvest takes in America's cities. Here bundles of poppy heads are sold openly at a street market in Phonsavan, Laos—no shame attached to the trade in what is seen as just another agricultural product.

and filtered, it is cooked again and ammonium chloride is added. This makes the morphine base sink to the bottom of the mixture. Repeated filtration and recooking, now with hydrochloric acid, let an ever-purer morphine base be manufactured. This is usually converted into heroin at a different laboratory. Generally, laboratories are built in isolated areas because they give off an unmistakable "pickle" smell, produced by the reaction of the morphine base when it is cooked with acetic anhydride.

The process of preparation is time-consuming, but the purer the

DRUG DIPLOMACY

When President Bush declared a war against terrorism in the aftermath of the Al Qaeda attacks of September 11, 2001, his first tangible target was Afghanistan and its Taliban rulers. As the bombs and missiles flew, so did the charge and the counter-charge from those who supported American actions and those who opposed them. Those who backed the U.S. pointed to what they said was the Taliban's leading role in Afghanistan's drug trade—a trade that had made the country the source for over 70 percent of the world's illicit opium.

Critics claimed that the notorious puritanism of the Taliban had extended to a hard line on drugs: had they not taken the unprecedented step of banning production throughout the country? The truth, as so often in such cases, lies somewhere in the middle: the Taliban were certainly by no means bad by the standards of recent Afghan rulers. On the other hand, their much-vaunted crackdown had clearly been conceived as an attempt to blackmail the West into recognizing their regime, their operations aimed not at stopping, but at controlling and taxing the traffickers for revenue.

product, the greater its worth and the easier it is to transport. Roughly, a kilo of cooked opium makes 10 grams of morphine base, which yields 5–6 grams of exportable heroin. Once it reaches the U.S., the heroin will then be "bulked out" again; heroin of this purity is unsafe to use. The need to **cut** it with other substances also lets street dealers make huge profits. Cutting also means contamination takes place. Many addicts have died due to the presence of toxic chemicals in what they believed to be "clean" heroin.

Afghanistan has been at war now for more than 20 years, and if the country is to stand any chance of ever being at peace again, it will have to be cured of its dependency on the drug trade and its related violence.

Cocaine

The 16th-century Italian navigator Amerigo Vespucci is most famous as the man who gave his name to the continents of North and South America, but he also makes a brief appearance in the history of drugs. In 1505, he wrote of his confusion on meeting men and women in the New World who chewed away for hours at a time on wads of an ordinary-looking green leaf. "They did this with much elaboration," he reported, "and the thing seemed wonderful, for we could not understand the secret, or with what object they did it." In fact, the natives of South America had been chewing coca leaves for at least 1,500 years before Amerigo's arrival, and his Spanish successors would quickly learn the secrets of this strange "green herb."

A stimulant, coca allows greater alertness and encourages endurance in spite of lack of sleep and food. The conquistadors would use it deliberately to increase the productivity of their Indian slaves. The fact that local populations have, for so many generations, regarded coca as an "old friend" has posed problems for modern attempts to control the trade in its more powerful derivative, cocaine. This drug has certainly been no friend to American society. Not only does it pose grave dangers in itself, but it has also given rise in recent times to a massive and murderous illegal trade.

THE DRUG BARONS

The emergence of the Colombian cartels has perhaps been the defining event of modern times as far as the drug trade is concerned. Oddly enough,

Left: Another three tons of cocaine are destroyed by the Colombian authorities; another blow is struck against the Calí cartel, but the *narcotraficantes'* profit margins are so astronomical that they can laugh at such reversals.

When chewed, as they have been for centuries by the Indians of the Andean region, coca leaves produce no more than a mildly stimulant buzz. A relatively complex chemical process is required for their manufacture into cocaine—and their preparation for a lucrative, and often violent, international trade.

though, Colombia has no long-term history of production. To begin with, Colombian smugglers specialized in smuggling jewels and cigarettes, and it was only in the late 1970s that they decided to move into drugs in a major way. Even then they operated first as smugglers rather than as producers, transporting cocaine that had been produced in Bolivia and Peru. As the market boomed in the 1980s, however, the Colombians were quick to realize the advantages of moving into production themselves. From the beginning, the boom in illegal drugs in Colombia was accompanied by a

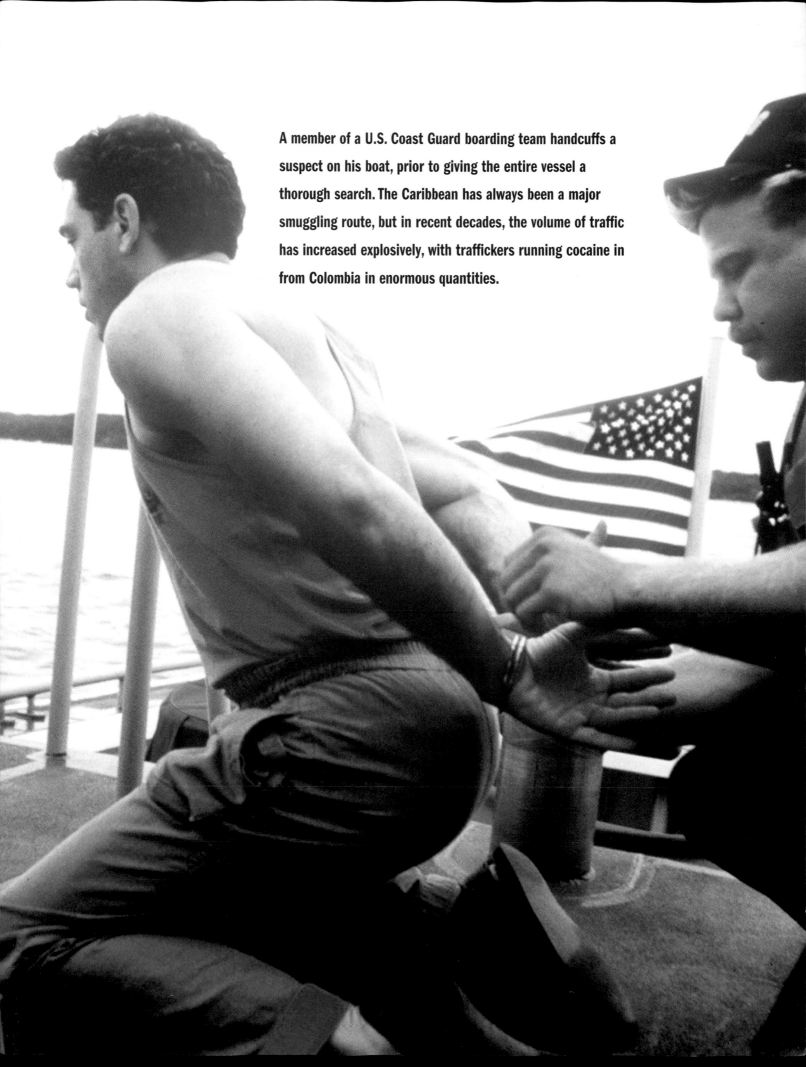

A member of a U.S. Coast Guard boarding team handcuffs a suspect on his boat, prior to giving the entire vessel a thorough search. The Caribbean has always been a major smuggling route, but in recent decades, the volume of traffic has increased explosively, with traffickers running cocaine in from Colombia in enormous quantities.

bust in law and order. Soon, the country had become the unrivaled murder capital of the world. The Western media has concentrated on the notorious power struggle between the competitive criminal forces of the Medellín and Cali cartels, and this has tended to ignore the fact that violence came to permeate every level of Colombian society.

This was the ugly background to the glamorous image cocaine had in American popular perceptions at the time. Already hooked on the money drugs brought in, many Colombians were soon addicted to the drugs themselves, especially when cheaper crack appeared on the market in the early 1980s. Gang leaders appreciated the life-and-death loyalty that crack dependence created in their armies of *sicarios*: teenage assassins often killed in a power struggle that claimed some 7,000 lives a year in Medellín alone.

THE RISE AND FALL OF PABLO ESCOBAR

Born in Medellín in 1949, Pablo Escobar is said to have had his start in crime by stealing headstones from the city cemetery. These would be sandblasted clean for resale to black-market buyers. After that, he went into auto crime: stealing and stripping cars for spare parts. Soon, he was doing this on an almost industrial scale. Along with a capacity for ruthless violence, this readiness to "think big" would be his making as an outlaw. His career as kidnapper began as a rough-and-ready method of debt collection. But Escobar did not stop there. He started kidnapping anyone whose family had the resources to pay a ransom.

In addition to big money, he gained a notoriety he had come to crave. A generous and giving man to the poor Medellín communities, whom he came to see as his "**constituency**," Escobar won a popular folk-hero status in which he reveled, conveniently disregarding the damage done by his evil trade.

As a cocaine smuggler, Escobar became one of the world's most famous men as well as one of its richest, but his arrogant attitude would eventually prove to be his undoing. While Escobar strutted his stuff before the world's

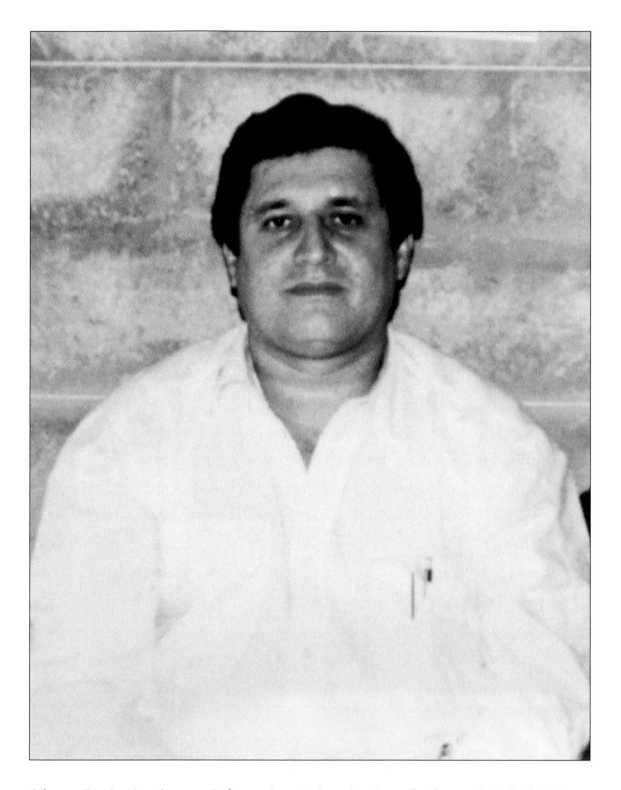

A former Escobar henchman and afterward a notorious drug baron in his own right, Fabio Ochoa was arrested with 30 followers in Medellín in October 1999. Ochoa's operation alone was shipping cocaine into the United States at a rate of some 20 tons a month: the total amounts being moved can hardly be guessed at.

press, his rivals in the Cali cartel were moving in on his empire, and his arrogance was infuriating the government in the United States, where his drugs were doing so much damage. As the U.S. authorities worked hard to have him extradited (brought to the U.S. to face charges), the Colombian government arrested and imprisoned him. A luxurious jail was built especially for him, fit to house the king of criminals. Yet, tiring even of these agreeable surroundings, Escobar escaped and went on the run. He was shot dead by Colombian law enforcement agents in 1993.

COLOMBIA'S CHRONIC PROBLEM

Andres Escobar (no relation of Pablo) was one of Colombia's foremost soccer stars. With him as the mainstay of the team, his countrymen assumed that they would sweep to victory in the 1994 World Cup. Having thrashed the much-admired Brazil in an earlier round, the Colombian team was expected to have no difficulty in disposing of the United States, but a huge error from poor Andres handed the match to the *yanquis* and saw Colombia knocked out of the tournament. Within 10 days, Escobar was dead, gunned down outside a Medellín nightclub. Rumors persisted that he had "thrown" the game deliberately, acting under orders from cartel members who had organized a profitable betting scheme around this wholly unexpected result.

We will never know the truth, but suspicion has poisoned every aspect of life in modern Colombia, a country in which everyone from politicians to priests are believed (at times correctly) to have been corrupted. Cocaine, blended with Colombian politics, has given the country a nasty problem: how can a country thrive when its leaders cannot be trusted? Moreover, the activities of the drug cartels have taken place in a country that is already suffering the effects of a long-standing civil war.

Ostensibly a "people's army," the Communist Revolutionary Armed Forces of Colombia (FARC) have little sympathy for their fellow Colombians, and are responsible for killing around 10,000 people every

Armed to the teeth for action, a Colombian antidrug soldier takes part in an operation, but a war will also have to be fought for the hearts and minds of local people. Currently, like it or not, their economic existence is bound up in the drug trade: they must be helped to find another way of life and kept safe to pursue it.

year. Operating largely in rural areas, massacring whole villages where they sense the slightest trace of resistance, the FARC has not been slow in getting in on the drug trafficking act. In addition to supervising production in the vast territories they control, they are believed to have cooperated with Bolivian and Peruvian groups in smuggling cocaine produced in guerrilla-occupied areas of those countries.

A PLAN FOR THE FUTURE

Supported by the United States, under its "Plan Colombia" program, the Colombian government has recently launched a major offensive against the FARC, pushing them out of large areas that were, until recently, off-limits to the authorities. With the help of satellite pictures, areas of coca cultivation have been identified and sprayed from the air (over 72,500 acres so far), while scores of processing labs have been discovered and destroyed. Shutting down laboratories "on the ground" is as crucial in the battle against cocaine smuggling as it is in the fight against heroin. As with the production of heroin, the progressive purification of cocaine involves a drastic reduction in total bulk, without which it would hardly make sense to smuggle the drug at all.

Dried out and then placed in a pit for treatment with kerosene or some other solvent, 100 kilos (220 pounds) of raw coca leaf yields only a kilo (2.2 pounds) of "cocaine base." This cocktail of cocaine sulfate and other compounds must then be treated with hydrochloric acid to produce some 350 grams (12 ounces) of cocaine hydrochloride powder—what an American buyer would recognize as usable "cocaine."

Many field producers in Peru and Bolivia take the process only to the point of cocaine base, which they then sell on to Colombian criminals for final processing and shipment to North America and Europe. Colombia is thus not only a major source in itself, but also a key staging post on the international cocaine highway. If the trade could be cut off here, it could be prevented almost completely.

So, while the U.S. authorities have worked with both Bolivia and Peru to stop cultivation and develop alternative economic strategies, Colombia has been the main focus of their efforts. And while the aggressive stamping out of production has been a priority, America has stuck to its pledge to offer alternative economic strategies for what are often very poor regions, providing active help with several major road- and bridge-building, water-supply, and sewage programs.

A soldier stands guard over sacks of cocaine confiscated during raids in the forests of Colombia: besides corrupting both the country's government and legal system, the drug trade has also helped finance the fighting through many wretched years of civil war.

Argentina's Diego Maradona (left) moves in as a teammate tackles a Nigerian player in an early round of the World Cup of 1994. Having already jeopardized his talents through cocaine use, Maradona saw his tournament end after he tested positive for performance-enhancing ephedrine.

CHILDREN OF ADDICTION

As crack, cocaine's "poor relation," tore through America's inner cities in the late 1980s, one single image seemed best to sum up the tragedy. Television viewers in America and worldwide were horrified to see the babies born 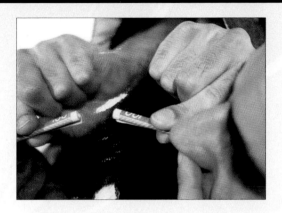 of this epidemic lying helpless in their incubators: underweight, stunted, sickly—and addicts from birth. Politicians and commentators were unanimous in their shock at the sight of these "crack babies," even though they did not necessarily share the same views on what the problem meant or how it might be dealt with. Drugs were a disease, said liberals, destroying the lives of the youngest and most innocent; the sins of the mothers, said sterner moralists, were being visited on the children. In fact, the direst prophecies have, for the most part, proved unfounded: cocaine in itself seems not to have harmed these children permanently, and, given the right conditions, "crack babies" can grow up as whole and healthy as any others. Their underdevelopment is now believed to result from other factors altogether, such as malnutrition or sexually transmitted diseases in their mothers, or their own impoverished existences after birth. Yet if crack cannot be held directly responsible for these babies' problems, it is quite clearly their indirect cause. When women sell their bodies and neglect their own care and nutrition in order to feed an insatiable addiction, there will inevitably be implications for any children they may bear.

The LSD Story

The war against drugs would be a difficult enough undertaking if it were simply a matter of destroying production and cutting off supplies. But it is not only drugs that have to be fought, but also an enormous "drug culture."

Ever since Coleridge conjured up the hallucinogenic world of his classic poem *Kubla Khan*—the faithful record, he claimed, of an opium dream—the connection has been made between taking drugs, "consciousness expansion," and creativity. This connection is debatable, to say the least. Such "inspiration" has little basis in reality, and for every talent supposedly set free by drugs, many more have been destroyed. And yet the assumption has persisted, reaching its height in the counterculture of the 1960s, with its outpouring of "psychedelic" art. Painting, poetry, and rock music all celebrated the effects of hallucinogenic drugs in letting loose the weird visions created by the unconscious mind.

LSD

No single substance better exemplified the psychedelic era than Lysergic Acid Diethethylamide, or LSD. The main purpose of the counterculture, a cynic might say in hindsight, was to exclude and offend an older generation that "couldn't understand," but the drugs were real, and they have left a lasting (and destructive) legacy.

Dr. Albert Hofmann and Dr. W.A. Stoll, researchers at the Sandoz Laboratories in Basel, Switzerland, first synthesized LSD in 1938. Since

Left: Hard rock, hard drugs—the music culture of the 1960s and 1970s is inextricably linked with psychedelic drugs. The use of drugs, in particular LSD, underscored the entire esthetic of those times—in music and writing, as well as in visual art.

they could find no obvious use for the new substance, which was derived from ergot, a grain fungus, it was simply set aside. Not until five years later did Hofmann decide to take a second look. Since the new substance had first been identified, applications for other ergot derivatives had been successfully developed, so it seemed natural to reopen the file on LSD.

Having worked with the substance for some time, Hofmann noticed that he was starting to feel dizzy; a few days later, he took a small dose deliberately and started recording his reactions. His journey home by bicycle has become one of the most famous bike rides ever: "My field vision swayed before me," he wrote, "and was distorted like the reflections in an amusement park mirror. The faces of those around me appeared as

Could this really have been Mom and Pop? Today the Woodstock Festival of 1969 seems to reflect an altogether alien and exotic culture, but for many thousands of young Americans, it was a drug-defining moment in their lives.

"Tune in, turn on, drop out," urged Timothy Leary in his own subversive State of the Union address; behind him, a poster shows President Lyndon B. Johnson's head on top of the body of the Nazi German dictator Adolf Hitler.

DAY TRIPPERS

Many thousands of young people throughout the world experimented with acid "trips" in the 1960s, and even for those who did not, LSD was central to the imagery of the time. Pop lyrics, album covers, and even "serious" works of art drew on the strange shapes, lurid colors, and crazy narrative logic LSD was known to produce in the hallucinating mind.

grotesque, colored masks. Sounds were transposed into visual sensations so that from each tone or noise, a comparable colored picture was evoked, changing in form and color kaleidoscopically."

The drug's extraordinary powers had now been established, but no use for it had yet been found. Experiments into possible applications in treating a number of psychiatric conditions, including schizophrenia, continued in the years that followed. The hope was that its obvious mind-altering properties might be channeled into altering distressed minds for the better. The drug was legal, but restricted by the Food and Drug Administration (FDA) to "investigative" uses. This was when Harvard researcher Timothy Leary began to use "acid" recreationally and to share it with friends and students, falling foul both of the law and the university authorities. Far from finding the official attention disconcerting, however, Leary used the notoriety he gained to issue his famous rallying cry to America's youth, urging them to "Tune in, turn on, drop out."

The more his call was heeded, unfortunately, the more the downside of LSD came to be revealed. There were several cases of people falling to their deaths from high windows, convinced that they could walk on air. For others, a "bad trip" turned out to be a positively hellish experience; some were permanently mentally damaged by the ordeal. Meanwhile, legitimate research was finding that it had reached a dead end. There was little sign of the hoped-for "miracle cure" for schizophrenia or other **psychoses**. In fact, the opposite seemed to be true. If anything, LSD seemed to make such conditions worse. In March 1966, President Johnson signed the Drug Abuse Control Amendment, banning LSD; the manufacturers at Sandoz bowed to the inevitable and withdrew it from the market. The drug has never gone away, however, and has indeed enjoyed something of a revival in recent years, finding a place alongside other synthesized drugs, such as ecstasy, on the rave and club scene.

A NEW WAVE OF DRUGS

While crack cocaine swept the streets of America's inner cities in the 1980s, middle-class students were taking a new wave of "designer drugs," designed specifically to give them a rush while keeping them on the right side of the law. Corrupt pharmacologists working in specialized laboratories, which were sometimes set up and then dismantled and moved after a single run, synthesized a range of substances whose molecular structure mimicked that of prohibited drugs without being identical. They produced similar sensations, but were not banned by legislation.

The Controlled Substance Analog Enforcement Act of 1986 extended existing bans to cover cases such as this, but by that time, arguably, the damage had already been done. One drug in particular had already sparked off the greatest explosion in drug use seen since the counterculture of the 1960s: methylenedioxymethamphetamine (MDMA), better known as ecstasy, or "E."

THE RAVE SCENE

Like LSD in the 1960s, ecstasy had an effect far beyond the **pharmacological**, becoming the defining drug of the "rave" culture of the 1990s. Types of music, styles of dress, modes of behavior, and attitudes to life—all were subsumed in a subculture for which the taking of "E" was the flagship fashion. In many ways, indeed, the ravers' "loved up" attitudes

THE ECSTASY AND THE AGONY

Ecstasy promotes a gentle feeling of contentment and goodwill in the user; but the bad news is that it has already claimed many lives worldwide. Taking ecstasy is a risky business. Deaths are sometimes attributed to contamination of the drug by unscrupulous or incompetent manufacturers, or individual takers' failure to follow established safety procedures (drinking lots of water, taking time out to "chill"). But the dangers do not end there. In fact, they may be just beginning: with such a new drug, we are only now starting to see some of the long-term consequences. Studies have shown that even in light recreational use, the drug impairs such essential functions of the brain as memory, learning, logical reasoning, and problem-solving. In short, using ecstasy is undeniably dangerous.

Here in Syracuse, New York, a clubber dances with glow sticks at an after-hours party: the rave scene has promoted drug use among a generation of young Americans who are otherwise entirely law-abiding, a fact that makes it difficult to combat.

could be seen to echo some of those of the hippies before them (often deliberately so), and these echoes were then picked up by the artists, designers, and musicians of the time.

For the most part, though, while ravers may have tuned in and turned on, they rejected Leary's final exhortation to "drop out," holding down respectable jobs and confining their drug outbreaks to weekends. Some '60s survivors have sneered at the ravers' respectability, and their indifference to the anti-establishment politics of the Hippy generation, but these things have paradoxically made them more difficult to deal with from the law enforcement point of view. An all-too-visible enemy, '60s drug-taking had at least the virtue of being a known quantity; it has been much harder for the authorities to get a handle on this more discreet and therefore far more elusive enemy.

The rave culture seems to have begun in England during the latter part of the 1980s. Young entrepreneurs began staging one-time only events in abandoned warehouses and factories, and sometimes in open fields. The live bands of yesteryear were now replaced by DJs playing electronic "techno" music; a well-organized event might even have specially designated chill-out areas with water laid out for rehydration. Alerted by word of mouth, young people would come flocking to what have aptly been described as "drug-taking festivals"—yet the connection between rave organizers and dealers was often maddeningly difficult for the authorities to prove in practice and therefore very difficult to combat.

By their very nomadic nature, raves could be all but impossible for police to keep track of: the same team would set up in a variety of venues, in different places in successive weeks. Even when police succeeded in locating a rave in progress, they might still find themselves facing an elusive enemy: most organizers made a great show of banning drugs, and drug dealers in particular, from their venues. This was no more than a fiction for the most part: even if such strictures had been sincere, they would have been very difficult to enforce. For young people, the attraction of raves was (and is today) due in large part to the availability of drugs. The reality was that organizers looked the other way while dealers sold drugs in discreet corners or stairways, or in parking lots outside. Such a "blind eye" policy is arguably the most dishonorable of all: many teenagers have now died as a result of drugs they have bought from dealers at such "drug-free" raves.

Here, a group of ravers dance through the night at an open-air event in Tel Aviv, Israel. The rave scene has become an integral part of youth culture throughout the world, and has developed its own language and music.

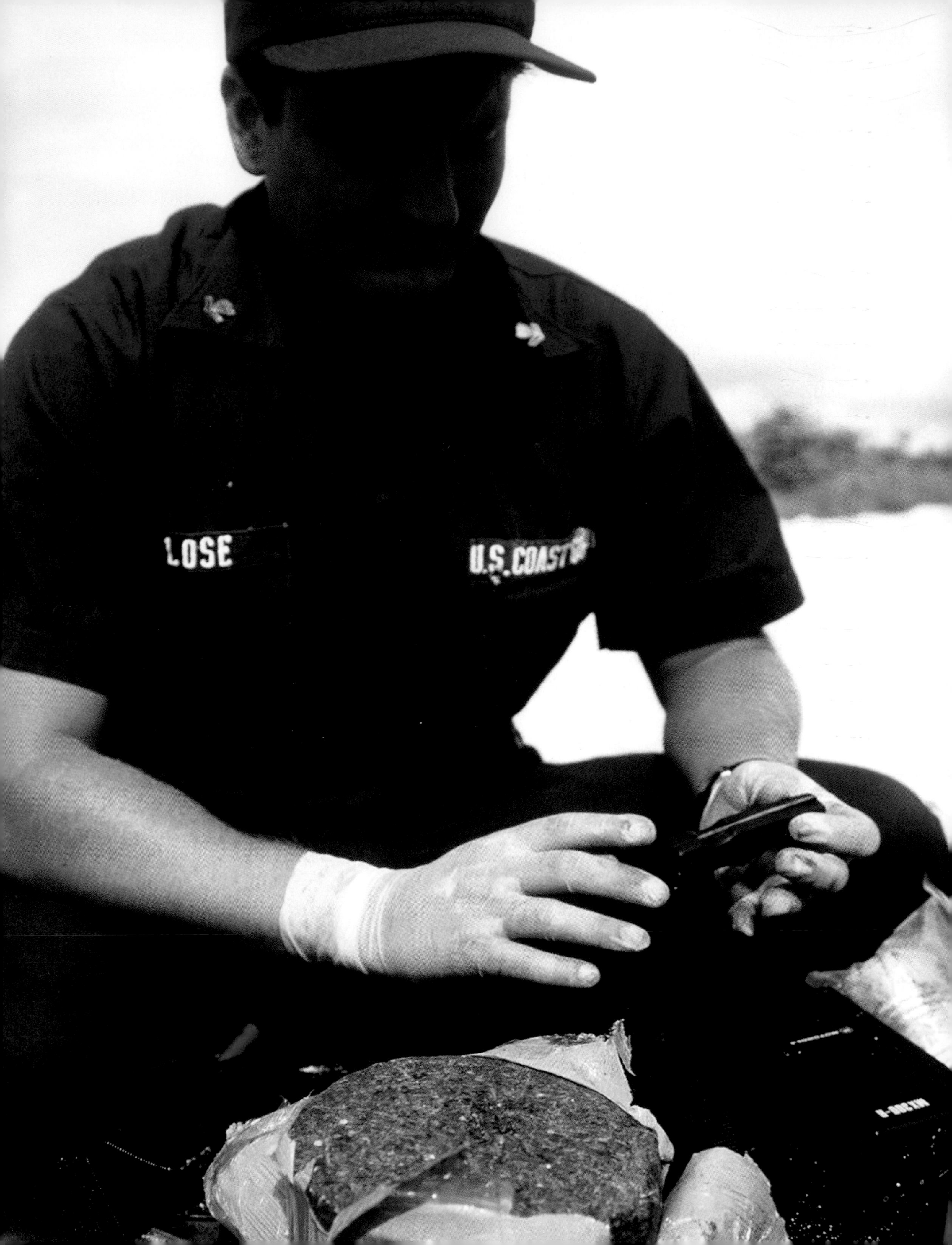

LOSE
U.S.COAST

The Battlefield

In waging the war against drugs, U.S. government agencies have had to fight on a number of fronts, from the Middle East to the Midwest, from Colombia to Columbus, Ohio. We owe much to those agencies in the firing line, from the Customs and Coast Guard to Border Patrol, as well as to law enforcement organizations from the FBI to local sheriffs' offices. At the same time, however, the chief responsibility for keeping America drug-free must rest with us, the people of America. Only if we set ourselves firmly enough against this threat will it finally be lifted from our communities.

Education can be crucial in enabling those who have become victims of drug abuse to take the first steps toward regaining their freedom and, perhaps as important, in stripping away the fake glamour so often attached to drugs in popular culture. Fortunately, many stars from the worlds of sports, fashion, music, and the movies have been prepared to contradict the widespread media message that drugs are cool, setting an inspiring example to their fans. There have been many initiatives in recent years attempting to reach out to young people and help them protect themselves against what can, at times, seem overwhelming pressures to go with the crowd. In the end, however, it is up to each and every one of us to hold our own.

STOPPING THE SMUGGLERS

In recent years, much of the emphasis in antidrug policy has been on restricting production in supplier countries, but there is still a clear place

Left: A member of the United States Coast Guard folds away his pocketknife after opening up a consignment of cannabis resin (or "hash"): government agencies intercept many thousands of such shipments every year.

When he died on the sidewalk outside a Hollywood nightclub on October 31, 1993, River Phoenix joined a long list of celebrities whose lives have been cut short by drugs. Unfortunately, such fatalities, far from discouraging interest in drugs, seem too often to lend them a romantic allure.

A team of Coast Guard officers searches a sailboat abandoned on a U.S. beach by suspected smugglers: the scale of profits means that successful drug runners can afford to write off just about any amount of expensive equipment.

for simply preventing illegal drug shipments from getting through. Every year, U.S. Custom officials working on our waterfronts and in our airports stop millions of dollars' worth of drugs from entering our country. In the process, they are potentially saving many lives. In 2001, the agency seized more than 1.5 million pounds (680, 395 kg) of marijuana nationally, along with around 190,000 pounds (86,185 kg) of cocaine and more than 3,500 pounds (1,588 kg) of heroin. Meanwhile, the Coast Guard patrols our inshore waters, looking for those hoping to land illegal drugs secretly. In recent years, it has seized an average of 135,000 pounds (61,235 kg) of cocaine and 67,000 pounds (30,390 kg) of marijuana per year.

The Border Patrol is generally charged with preventing the entry of illegal immigrants, most of whom have come simply to work. Down the decades, however, many of those apprehended have proved to be smuggling goods along with them, and this has increased in recent years. Today, the Border Patrol sees stopping the flow of drugs as a major part of its work. All these agents can hope to do, however, is to bear down on illegal imports brought in by ruthless, resourceful, and well-funded smugglers.

One method for smuggling drugs is to use a human "mule." A drug can be wrapped in a rubber condom and then swallowed by the "mule," to be brought into a country undetected in the stomach. Drugs may be flown into remote forest clearings in light aircraft or brought in fast powerboats to be landed on isolated beaches. A hollowed-out car door, a metal bar, the heel of a shoe, or a delivery of grain can all be used to conceal a shipment of drugs. Determined traffickers will always find a way to transport drugs.

THE FIGHT FOR THE STREETS

The agency primarily charged with the task of tackling the problem of illegal drugs within America is the Drug Enforcement Administration (DEA), but its officials work in conjunction with many different law enforcement and other administrative agencies. Operations are mounted in cooperation with the FBI, state and city police departments, and sheriffs'

Here, U.S. Coast Guard Tactical Law Enforcement Team members unload bales of cocaine inside the hold of the Panamanian registered vessel, *Castor*. More than 10,000 lbs (4,500 kg) of cocaine was found on board the vessel off the coast of Florida. The drug bust was an interagency effort that ended with the Coast Guard cutter *Decisive* escorting the *Castor* to Miami.

Home economics for a lost generation: cocaine mixed with water and baking powder is cooked on an ordinary kitchen ring to produce dry "rocks" of crack. In this smokeable form, the drug proves powerfully addictive and devastatingly damaging to health.

offices, as well as with other national agencies, like Customs, Coast Guard, and Border Patrol, and also overseas governments where appropriate.

In one typical operation staged in October 2001, the DEA collaborated with field offices throughout the country as well as with state and local law

AGENT AXEL

A German Shepherd-Rottweiler mix, Axel is a genius when it comes to sniffing out hidden drugs. Once, he found a shipment hidden at the heart of a truckload of fragrant—and prickly—pineapples. Officially a "Narcotics Detection Canine," he works with the FBI in New York City, and can recognize no fewer than six different illegal substances by scent. Axel earns his keep many times over every year. In 1997 alone, he found drugs with a street value of over 25 million dollars.

enforcement offices in the state where the actual raid was mounted: Escondido, California. Over 40,000 ecstasy tablets were seized, as well as large quantities of related chemicals, lab equipment, and weaponry. They also seized $429,000 in cash, which was then put directly into further antidrug projects.

While the federal agencies get the headlines, the work of local law enforcement officers is of immense importance. They deal with drug dealing and drug-related crime on a daily basis. Such

President George W. Bush recognizes his own generation's role in popularizing drugs (and is himself a former alcoholic). "One of the interesting questions facing baby boomers," he has said, "is have we grown up? Are we willing to share the wisdom of past mistakes?"

Two young Americans walking home from school chat with their local cop: life will not always be as easy and untroubled as it seems now. So long as they can stay free of drugs, though, they will be free to live the happy and fulfilled lives that is every American's birthright.

SPORTS, NOT DRUGS

Congo-born basketball player and Philadelphia '76ers star Dikembe Mutombo has decided to give something back both to his fans in the U.S. and the kids back in Africa. As a Youth Emissary for the United Nations, he has taken part in a worldwide campaign calling on young people to think harder about their role in their home communities. In America, he believes, no problem is more pressing than that of illegal drugs, a problem ravaging communities almost as badly as AIDS has been doing in his native Africa. Wherever they are in the world, young people have a part to play in building the destiny of their communities. As the grown-ups of the future, the lives of all the nations are in their hands.

From sports stars to singers and supermodels, personalities of all kinds have come to recognize their status as role models for the young, and their responsibilities toward the thousands of young fans whose admiration sustains their celebrity. More and more in recent years, they have been prepared to stand up and speak out against the evils of illegal drugs, driving home the message that success is about staying clean and able, not about muddling your mind or destroying your body. Critics often sneer at programs of this kind, claiming that they are ways for publicity-mad personalities to gain yet more coverage, but such objections are wrong. In bringing the war against drugs down to the level of individual celebrity, these stars reinforce the vital message that, ultimately, our first line of resistance to the drug menace must be our self-image and self-respect. When all is said and done, and despite the valuable work of the various enforcement agencies or educational programs throughout society, our best protection against drugs must remain ourselves.

RED RIBBON WEEK

Red Ribbon Week was originally introduced to celebrate the life of DEA Special Agent Enrique Camarena of Imperial Valley, California, after his death in the line of duty in 1985. Since then, it has become the centerpiece of the antidrug calendar, with rallies, promotional programs, street events, and the wearing of red ribbons. But for many young people in America, Red Ribbon Week lasts all year, through associated activities in schools and community centers. "For me, it has been something huge, something major in my life. If it wasn't for this club, I wouldn't be drug-free," was the frank admission of Nancy Granados, president of Calexico High School's Red Ribbon Club. Another student representative, Maritza Briceno, put it more starkly still: "Living an antidrug life is actually realizing that you have a life, it's choosing to live."

firsthand experience is often of key significance. Indeed, they play an essential role as the "eyes and ears" of federal agencies, whose officers are inevitably removed from most of the action that unfolds daily on the streets.

Ordinary people have a part to play, too, not only in reporting what they see and hear to the authorities, but also in avoiding any involvement with drugs themselves. However hard our antitrafficking and law enforcement agencies work, they will never be able stop the trade in drugs completely while demand exists among the population.

EDUCATION

In the end, we can protect ourselves as a nation only if we each take responsibility for protecting ourselves, but we need education to equip us for the task. We need to understand not only how dangerous drugs can be, but also how exciting and fulfilling our lives can be without them. Hence, the activities of community-education programs in the most deprived neighborhoods. Here, too, many young people often do not see that they have anything in their lives to strive for. Drug use seems to offer a quick way out of a depressing situation, though in reality, it condemns those at the bottom of the social heap to stay where they are. Programs from sports training to the formation of other activity groups, such as the Harlem Boys and Girls Choirs, enable young people accustomed since birth to the idea of failure to realize that they have worthwhile talents and ambitions.

For other young people, though, drugs are not about desperation, but about aspiration. They want to do things they associate with the lifestyles of the rich and famous. This is where programs like the auto sports industry's "Race Against Drugs" campaign come in, spreading the message that drugs are the enemy of the winner, not the glamorous badge of the victor.

Here, on June 26, 2002, the Chinese city of Guangzhou marks International Antidrug Day with a display of drugs that were seized on the border with Hong Kong and Macau.

GLOSSARY

Addict: someone who is physically or psychologically dependent on a drug

AIDS (Acquired Immune Deficiency Syndrome): an illness caused by HIV (Human Immunodeficiency Virus), which compromises the body's built-in defenses against infection by all sorts of other diseases

Alcoholism: addiction to alcohol

Constituency: the people involved in or served by an organization

Cut: to mix a drug with other substances; this is usually done by the dealers, who dillute the drugs in order to increase profits

Debilitate: to weaken, make feeble

Endorphins: any of a group of proteins with potent analgesic properties that occur naturally in the brain

Euphoria: a feeling of well-being or elation

Hallucinogen: a substance that causes people to see or hear things that are not there

"Hard" and "soft" drugs: a distinction drawn between highly potent and extremely addictive drugs, like cocaine and heroin, and those thought to be milder and less harmful in their effects, such as marijuana

Illicit: unlawful

Intravenous: situated, performed, or occurring within or entering by way of a vein

Machete: a large, heavy knife

Paranoia: a tendency toward excessive or irrational suspiciousness and distrustfulness of others

Pharmacological: of or relating to the science of drugs, particularly their uses and effects

Physiological: of or relating to how the body functions

Psychosis: any mental disorder that is so severe it distorts the affected person's contact with reality

Sedative: a drug that causes a person to feel calm or soothed

Soma: an intoxicating plant juice derived from a leafless vine of the milk-weed family

Trafficker: a person who trades in illicit goods

CHRONOLOGY

c. 8000 B.C.: Hemp seeds are discovered in excavations at Neolithic sites in east and central Europe, suggesting that the use of marijuana may be just about as old as civilization.

c. 1000: Some of the oldest known writings in the world, found at Sumerian sites in the Middle East, celebrate the poppy as the "plant of joy," although its properties had almost certainly been known for many centuries previously; the chewing of coca by native peoples in South America is believed to be of similar antiquity.

A.D. 1684: English apothecary (a chemist or druggist) Thomas Sydenham places laudanum on the market, a solution of opium in sherry with herbs; sold as a pain-relieving medicine, it soon catches on more widely, remaining legal despite the addiction of users at every level of society.

1727: Chinese emperor Yung Cheng prohibits opium-taking in his territories, sparking over a century of friction and finally open conflict with Western merchants and their governments.

1798: English poet Samuel Taylor Coleridge writes his poem *Kubla Khan*, the record of an opium dream; he was addicted to the drug, which he took in the form of laudanum.

1839–1842: First "Opium War" between Britain and China.

1856–1860: Second "Opium War."

1868: Pharmacy Act.

1875–1890: Legislation is enacted closing down opium dens in western states.

1914: Harrison Narcotics Act.

1930: Federal Bureau of Narcotics (FBN) is founded.

1938: Lysergic Acid Diethylamide (LSD) is first synthesized.

1951:   Boggs Act.

1956:   Narcotic Control Act.

1965:   Bureau of Drug Abuse Control (BDAC) is formed within the Food and Drugs Administration (FDA).

1966:   President Johnson signs the Drug Abuse Control Amendment, banning LSD.

1968:   BDAC merges with the FBN to form the Bureau of Narcotics and Dangerous Drugs (BNDD).

1973:   All federal antidrug forces are brought together into the Drug Enforcement Administration (DEA).

1980s: Emergence of Colombian cartels as key players on the international drug-smuggling scene; the waning of the fashion for cocaine among the professional elite leads to the introduction of cheaper and more dangerous crack.

1986:   Controlled Substance Analog Enforcement Act outlaws "designer drugs."

2000:   "Plan Colombia" is launched, a cooperative venture by the U.S. with Andres Pastrana's Colombian government, with the dual aim of stamping out cocaine production and providing alternative economic possibilities for regions dependent on earnings from the drugs trade.

2001:   Former U.S. Attorney and congressman Asa Hutchinson becomes DEA Administrator.

2002:   Mexican drug boss Benjamin Arellano Felix is finally captured in Mexico after 10 years on the DEA's "most wanted" list; his brother Ramon is killed in a shoot-out by Mexican police.

FURTHER INFORMATION

Useful Web Sites

Department of Justice Web site: www.usdoj.gov

Immigration and Naturalization Service Web site: www.ins.usdoj.gov

U.S. Customs Web site: www.customs.ustreas.gov

Coast Guard Web site: www.uscg.mil.

Drug Enforcement Administration Web site: www.usdoj.gov/dea

Further Reading

Bowden, Mark. *Killing Pablo: The Hunt for the World's Greatest Outlaw*. New York: Atlantic Monthly Press, 2001.

Davies, Luke. *Candy: A Novel of Love and Addiction*. New York: Ballantine Books, 1998.

Fernandez, Humberto. *Heroin, Center City*. Minnesota: Hazelden Information Education, 1998.

Flynn, John C. *Cocaine: An In-Depth Look at the Facts, Science, History and Future of the World's Most Addictive Drug*. New York: Citadel Press, 1993.

Gately, Iain. *Tobacco: A Cultural History of How An Exotic Plant Seduced Civilization*. New York: Grove Press, 2002.

Gootenberg, Paul (ed.). *Cocaine: Global Histories*. New York: Routledge, 1999.

Streatfeild, Dominic. *Cocaine: An Unauthorised Biography*. London: Virgin, 2001.

About the Author

Michael Kerrigan was born in Liverpool, England, and educated at St. Edward's College, from where he won an Open Scholarship to University College, Oxford. He lived for a time in the United States, spending time first at Princeton, followed by a period working in publishing in New York. Since then he has been a freelance writer and journalist, with commissions across a very wide range of subjects, but with a special interest in social policy and defense issues. Within this field, he has written on every region of the world.

His work has been published by leading international educational publishers, including the BBC, Dorling Kindersley, Time-Life, and Reader's Digest Books. His work as a journalist includes regular contributions to the Times Literary Supplement, London, as well as a weekly column in the Scotsman newspaper, Edinburgh, where he now lives with his wife and their two small children.

INDEX